YOUR KNOWLEDGE HAS VALUE

- We will publish your bachelor's and master's thesis, essays and papers

- Your own eBook and book - sold worldwide in all relevant shops

- Earn money with each sale

Upload your text at www.GRIN.com
and publish for free

Bibliographic information published by the German National Library:

The German National Library lists this publication in the National Bibliography; detailed bibliographic data are available on the Internet at http://dnb.dnb.de .

This book is copyright material and must not be copied, reproduced, transferred, distributed, leased, licensed or publicly performed or used in any way except as specifically permitted in writing by the publishers, as allowed under the terms and conditions under which it was purchased or as strictly permitted by applicable copyright law. Any unauthorized distribution or use of this text may be a direct infringement of the author s and publisher s rights and those responsible may be liable in law accordingly.

Imprint:

Copyright © 2016 GRIN Verlag
Print and binding: Books on Demand GmbH, Norderstedt Germany
ISBN: 9783668632707

This book at GRIN:

https://www.grin.com/document/411973

Jan-David Franke

Aus der Reihe: e-fellows.net stipendiaten-wissen

e-fellows.net (Hrsg.)

Band 2667

What has been the impact of national self-determination on the international system?

GRIN Verlag

GRIN - Your knowledge has value

Since its foundation in 1998, GRIN has specialized in publishing academic texts by students, college teachers and other academics as e-book and printed book. The website www.grin.com is an ideal platform for presenting term papers, final papers, scientific essays, dissertations and specialist books.

Visit us on the internet:

http://www.grin.com/

http://www.facebook.com/grincom

http://www.twitter.com/grin_com

What has been the impact of national self-determination on the international system?

By Jan-David Franke | HT16

"Nation, nationality, nationalism – all have proved notoriously difficult to define, let alone to analyse", Anderson (2006, p.3) writes somewhat consternated before trying to change just that in about two-hundred pages. In this essay, I shall have a go at the principle of national self-determination in about a fiftieth of the space and sketch its impact on the international system. For that purpose, I will first establish a neo-realist conception of the international system and define national self-determination to then go on and delineate how the latter has hurt the former. By looking at two historical cases, Nazi-Germany and decolonization, I will focus on the way self-determination highlights the independent significance of norms in international order, undermines the balance of power and – while seemingly cementing an international Westphalian system of stable states – is a continuous force of disruption within it.

The international system

When thinking about the defining aspects of a system, not only in the context of International Relations, three key points are absolutely essential:

a. What is a system?

b. What are its units?

c. What are the mechanisms and principles governing it?

In contrast to random co-existence a system delineates "a set of things working together as parts of a mechanism or an interconnecting network" (Oxford Dictionaries, n.d.). Neo-realists like Waltz (1979) believe that these 'things' on an international stage are states. It is not that they do not recognize the existence of sub-state actors but they simply do not credit them with enough independent power to compromise the parsimony of a state-based approach. The governing principle in this world of states is anarchy: the pursuit of competitive, self-interest in the absence of central authority. As Krasner (1995, p.1) points out, neo-realists assume the Westphalian model in their conception of the international system, which is premised on sovereign, autonomous, states with exclusive authority over clearly bounded territory. Neo-realists further emphasize the distribution of power as a defining characteristic of the system and state behavior. Normative aspects are but epiphenomena of power and interest. Rather, every state's elementary interest is to further its own security and it seeks to curtail foreign power and enhance its own in pursuit of that end. In order to find security in a grim world of aggression, states establish and participate in a balance-of-power mechanism that ought to prevent individual actors from becoming too strong or aggressive. States can balance power internally by developing capabilities themselves with which to check potential aggression or externally by building alliances, threatening or waging war and negotiating "territorial compensations or partitions for the purposes of redistributing the sources of power" (Levy, 2004, p.35).

National self-determination

National self-determination rests on the proposition "that the nation can only be protected, fulfilled, and developed within its state", as Hurrell (2007, p.123) says. According to him, the principle of national self-determination has manifested itself in three forms: political ideology, international political norm and international legal norm. As a political ideology, it posits that every nation needs a territorially congruous state that expresses its national idea, as a political norm, it "confers political and moral rights on national groups or on those speaking in their name" (ibid., p.126) and it has normative legal character in that it constitutes a peremptory principle of international law. The first three stipulations of the Atlantic Charter (1941) and the UN General Assembly Resolution 1514 (1960), just two prevalent examples of many, prescribe the right to national self-determination. The latter, quite interestingly so, was adopted by the General Assembly to endorse the independence of (former) colonies, a context that I shall return to in the course of this essay.

National self-determination is closely linked to broader national sentiments. What differentiates it from nationalism is that the latter amends the underlying symbiosis of nation and state with ontological claims about the natural legitimacy of a world of nations, the particular character immanent in each single nation and the supremacy of national loyalty (Hurrell, 2007, p.123). However, while attempts to curtail the threat that nationalist ideologies pose to international society, for instance, are well-advised to differentiate between nationalism and self-determination, Hurrell internalizes the lack of discriminatory power when faced with factual, outcome-related differences between them. Conceding to a 'notorious difficulty' to define and differentiate national sentiment, more often than not he uses the terms interchangeably. However, as both nationalism and national self-determination entail similar problems for the neo-realist conception of the international system, I will not unnecessarily dwell upon the matter.

How national self-determination hurts the neo-realist conception of the international system

In this section, I will show how the principle of national self-determination not only underscores the independent significance of norms but also threatens the neo-realist conception of the international system and of international security by undermining the balance of power and constituting a continuous force of disruption to Westphalian stability.[1] Two historical cases of national self-determination, Nazi-Germany and decolonization, will help to exemplify my points.

For a neo-realist, the dissolution of European empire after World War II is easily explained by looking at altered material capabilities after the war. Financial and military exhaustion facilitated "shifts in the relative balance of power between center and periphery" (Spruyt, 2000,

---

[1] This discussion could be more complex when accounting for different kinds of polarity. Unfortunately, that exceeds the necessary scope of this paper.

p.66) and so colonial powers were either not powerful enough to retain imperial influence or did not regard it in their immediate material interest anymore to do so. However, Spruyt, as have others before him (cp. Finnemore, 1993; Goertz, 1994; Finnemore & Sikkink, 1998; Tan, 2015), makes a very compelling case that there is to more to the dynamics of decolonization than meets the positivist eye. He argues that it was not normative changes in the European imperial centers that facilitated the end of empire (cp. Porter & Stockwell, 1989; Albertini, 1971; Mommsen, 1990), a common normative explanation that gives the colonial powers a form of moral agency they did not possess[2]. Rather, it was the 'peripheral' countries embracing the principle of national self-determination, not only independently of the distribution of power but in direct opposition to it, that led to widespread autonomization from the imperial yoke. The case of decolonization shows that if norms maintain internal consistency, there are incentives for political leaders to champion them and the international environment is forbearing if not charitable, they carry strong causal force in political change (Spruyt, 2007, p.88). National self-determination in the colonial context constituted an internally coherent idea of unification in contrast to European otherness, offered strategic advantages for political elites in the case of fulfilled independence, and was seen charitably not only by the anti-imperialist poles of the Cold War but also by the larger non-European-empires international community. The UN General Assembly 1514 bears testimony to that.

In bringing sovereign, territorial rule to the 'Third World' the principle of national self-determination created the modern state system and extended the Westphalian order across the globe, Spruyt concludes (ibid.). After all, the political elites in newly independent former colonies have a particular interest in the centrality of the state in the international system, Ayoob observes (1995, p.25). However, the principle of national self-determination, while seemingly cementing and legitimating an international Westphalian order, is a source of ongoing disruption to and instability within it. As Anderson writes "many 'old nations', once thought fully consolidated, find themselves challenged by 'sub'-nationalisms within their borders, nationalisms which, naturally, dream of shedding this sub-ness one day" (2006, p.3). By continuously 'encouraging and legitimizing demands for the redrawing of state boundaries' (Hurrell, 2007, p.126), national self-determination can lead into virtually infinite regress, by which instead of establishing sovereignty and territorial boundaries it questions and undermines them evermore[3]. In doing so, self-determination threatens the relative state-based stability of the neo-realist international system (ibid., p.130; Kedourie, 1984, p.354), constituting a normative and transformative nuisance to Westphalia. In recognition of that fact, the member states of the Organization of African Unity (OAU), predecessor to the African Union,

---

[2] "Imperial capitals and populations were relatively untroubled with the moral rectitude of empire" (Spruyt, 2000, p.66). Looking at the historical amnesia that is characteristic of the United Kingdom and of this university in particular, it is apparent that, sadly, not all times are a-changing.

[3] In Europe alone and only at this very point in time, national self-determination has disruptive force in the context of Scotland, the Basque region, Catalonia, Ukraine, Northern Italy, Kosovo as well as Cyprus, and that is not even to mention its ideological impact on right-wing movements and on the broader framework of European integration.

declared to "respect the borders existing on their achievement of national independence" (OAU, 1964, AHG/Res. 16[I]) to nip further attempts of self-determination in the bud (Hurrell, 2007, pp.126-127). It is no accident that attempts were commonly made in international law to narrow both scope and connotation of the *jus cogens* that is self-determination so as to not let it harm the realist[4] order of the world. While nationalist sentiment, ironically so, is in some way an ideological response to one axiom of neo-realism, international anarchy, its prevalence has constituted a departure from another: pluralist statehood (Hurrell, 2007, p.121).

Self-determination also threatens the neo-realist conception of the international system of order and stability by undermining its primary security mechanism: the balance of power. The case of an evermore aggressive Nazi-Germany in the late 1930s exemplifies how the principle weakened both internal and external power-balancing and thereby helped to enable the horrors of World War II (Hurrell, 2007). Not only did the nationalist rhetoric of 'a common people under a common state' legitimize the German project to bring Austria, Czechoslovakia and Poland *heim ins Reich* and thereby obfuscated the extent of its aggression and the decisiveness of external counter-balancing (cp. Rock, 2000). Also, a fragmented Central Europe, partially caught up in early nationhood[5], weak and non-viable, was hardly capable of internally developing capabilities which to even marginally check German expansion (Hurrell, 2007, p.130). Beyond the case of Germany, self-determination has fundamentally complicated another crucial mechanism of external power-balancing by propagating an ideological exaltation of the nation that forbids the concession of territory. Furthermore, it has "made conflicts all the more savage and destructive now that what is at stake is the control of a state apparatus, and the enormous power such control is seen to confer" (Kedourie, 1984, p.354).

Conclusion

In this essay, I have argued that national self-determination poses a threat to a neo-realist conception of the international system. For that purpose, I have defined that conception and the mechanisms it presupposes as well as the principle of national self-determination in its various manifestations. I have then tried to show how self-determination brings to light the independent causal force of normative factors in the international system. Eventually, while it appears to establish and cement a stable, international order of states, it in fact causes continuous disruption to the Westphalian system by threatening an infinite regress of nationalist disintegration and undermining the balance of power. The principle of national self-determination reveals the overly parsimonious impracticality (or imprecision) of the neo-realist international system. However, given that "national self-determination is a problem for overtly liberal understandings of order and, in particular, for democratic peace theory" (Hurrell, 2007,

---

[4] For the sake of being concise, I equate 'pluralist' with 'realist' here. Although there are marginal differences, they are of little consequence for my argument.
[5] Ayoob (1995) argues in the context of decolonization that an eminent cause of Third World insecurity is the early phase of nation-building that many postcolonial states find themselves in and compares it to the European experience.

p.132) and "represents Marxism's great historical failure" (Nairn, as cited in Anderson, 2000, p.3) suggests that neo-realism is not the only theory of International Relations that has fallen prey to its 'notorious difficulty'.

Bibliography

Albertini, R. (1971). *Decolonization: the administration and future of the colonies, 1919-1960.* Garden City, NY: Doubleday.

Anderson, B. (2006). *Imagined Communities.* London: Verso.

Atlantic Charter. (1941). Retrieved February 26, 2016, from http://avalon.law.yale.edu/wwii/atlantic.asp

Ayoob, M. (1995). *The third world security predicament.* London: Lynne Rienner Publishers.

Finnemore, M. (1993). International organizations as teachers of norms: the United Nations educational, scientific, and cultural organization and science policy. *International Organization, 47*(4), 565-597.

Finnemore, M., & Sikkink, K. (1998). International norm dynamics and change. *International Organization, 52*(4), 887-917.

Goertz, G. (1998). The norm of decolonization. In G. Goertz (Ed.), *Contexts of international politics* (pp. 250-267). Cambridge: Cambridge University Press.

Hurrell, A. (2007). Nationalism and the politics of identity. In A. Hurrell (Ed.), *On global order: power, values, and the constitution of international society* (Ch. 5). Oxford: Oxford University Press.

Kedourie, E. (1984). A new international disorder. In H. Bull & A. Watson (Eds.), *The expansion of international society,* (pp. 347-357). Oxford: Oxford University Press.

Krasner, S. (1995). Compromising Westphalia. *International Security, 20*(3), 115-151.

Levy, J. (2004). What do great powers balance against and when? In T. Paul, J. Wirtz & M. Fortmann, *Balance of power: theory and practice in the 21st century,* (pp. 29-51). Stanford: Stanford University Press.

Mommsen, W. (1990). Das Ende der Kolonialreiche. Dekolonisation und die Politik der Großmächte. Fischer.

Organization of African Unity. (1964). *Resolutions adopted by the first ordinary session of the assembly of heads of state and government.* Retrieved February 27, 2016, from http://www.au.int/en/sites/default/files/decisions/9514-assembly_en_17_21_july_1964_assembly_heads_state_government_first_ordinary_session.pdf

Porter, A., & Stockwell, A. (1989). *British imperial policy and decolonization, 1938-1964.* London: Palgrave Macmillan UK.

Rock, S. (2000). British appeasement of Germany, 1936-1939. In S. Rock (Ed.), *Appeasement in international politics,* (pp.49-77). Lexington: University Press of Kentucky.

Spruyt, H. (2000). The end of empire and the extension of the Westphalian system: the normative basis of the modern state order. *International Studies Association, 2*(2), 65-92.

System. (n.d.). *Oxford Dictionaries.* Retrieved February 26, 2016, from http://www.oxforddictionaries.com/definition/english/system

Tan, L. (2015). Rethinking the role of ideas and norms in twentieth century decolonization: constructing metropolitan British identities and responding to Indian nationalism (1929- 1935). *Intenational Relations, 29*(2), 177-197.

United Nations. (1960). General Assembly resolution 1514 (XV): declaration on the granting of independence to colonial countries and peoples.

Waltz, K. (1979). *Theory of international politics.* Reading, MA: Addison-Wesley Pub. Co.

YOUR KNOWLEDGE HAS VALUE

- We will publish your bachelor's and master's thesis, essays and papers

- Your own eBook and book - sold worldwide in all relevant shops

- Earn money with each sale

Upload your text at www.GRIN.com and publish for free